Ibrahim Ali Khadim is an Emirati writer and researcher, who has managed notable "Tarjim" and "Oktub" initiatives, works in content development, publication, and translation. In the public sector, he has made numerous contributions.

Ibrahim's role as Director of Media Content in the United Arab Emirates contributes to the development of the sector.

These pages are dedicated to all of the incredible, inspiring, loving, believers in the power of life.

Ibrahim Ali Khadim

TEACHINGS OF LOVE

Inspirational Principles of Lifelong Love

AUSTIN MACAULEY PUBLISHERS™

LONDON * CAMBRIDGE * NEW YORK * SHARJAH

ISBN – 9789948831051 – (Paperback)
ISBN – 9789948831068 – (E-Book)

Application Number: MC-10-01-5205157
Age Classification: E

First Published 2021
AUSTIN MACAULEY PUBLISHERS FZE
Sharjah Publishing City
P.O Box [519201]
Sharjah, UAE
www.austinmacauley.ae
+971 655 95 202

1

Take it easy…you'll never believe, after all, how complicated you were.

You've got an extraordinary ability to complicate simple things. You weave threads and create your own knots of worries, only to realize that these are self-created. You are eventually bewildered and regretful when you forget where you started and where you left the knots of worry in the yarn of thoughts, fears, and illusions.

****

Why do you complicate things like that?

Maybe you do so because we carry within ourselves two conflicting powers; the power of the soul and the power of the self. It seems as if your own self is drawn into the interpretation of everything and you inevitably enter into the depths of others only to find yourself sinking in suspicion but then, the purity of your soul rejects these thoughts as it is a breath from the sky that started with peace.

If you were the one who chose to entertain the rebellious gladiator inside you, then he will provoke a raging fire within you, silencing the voice of truth that your soul speaks. Even if you thought that no one would overcome you, once you are free from the consequences of your actions, only then can you truly realize how simple it was from the beginning but this would not be possible had it not been for the destruction that opened your eyes.

****

Now, the time has come to take it easy and follow the voice of wisdom. Live your life to the fullest in the present and do not be disturbed by the complicated past, or the future that shines unseen.

Just start with your beautiful heart and receive all thoughts with limitless love until you diffuse the fear that exists within you and is engulfed by the tranquil calmness that transcends from wisdom.

****

Then, you will learn well from your experience and you can certainly believe how unwise you were when you complicated things. You will be able to see in hindsight how right you are when you leave the intricate nets of every relationship, thought, or concern loose and free.

Soon, you will realize that life loves us when we make it simple and live cheerfully with joy, but it worries us when we waste and exhaust ourselves over petty matters that consume and render us insubstantial.

****

2

Do not get excessive...do not despise small matters!

We were created this way; we want the whole of everything, and we complain when we get little.

We accept only full attention from others and if we don't get it, we consider them to be disregarding and their attitude toward us unfair.

After that, we chase those small matters that gradually begin to disappear.

****

We may then get what we want but do not know how much of it we need and for how long! We may return to the empty circle of greed and attention and remain hard-hearted, thinking that power lies in wanting to have everything by clinging to it tooth and nail, so as not to let anything escape us. We then become confused and grieved, reluctantly wishing to let go of our obstinacy.

Ease your poor heart, you have burdened it; do not exaggerate and do not neglect anything. It starts with you first, with an easy step. Those who thought that the attainment of a thing had to be only in full have perished; the blessing is in the easy little things, as it is in our hands and before our eyes.

****

If you were worried about the size of your giving, such generosity will lose value as it comes from a miserly heart and will not reach the recipient in due time and good condition.

On the other hand, if you give with good and pure intent, you will have more rewards and the beneficiary will highly value what you gave no matter how small the offering. So, do not despise or undervalue what you give!

****

You know how much negligence you caused yourself when you missed the chances of giving and for saving without good reason? Nonetheless, you still have time. Very soon, you will thank the waiter with a simple word 'thank you' which is often hard to say.

You will pay more attention and give more care to the ones you love, though they may never reiterate the same sentences and words for you.

****

3

Learn how to have control over your intentions before you speak out.

Sometimes, they call it an idea while others think it is suspicion that forms an idea. However, you know well that despite the differences, it made you determined that you would not forgive and deeply admit that you neglected and even went farther beyond the normal reaction.

****

Misgivings have misled and destroyed us since the time of the fierce battles until the people trespass the inviolability of one another; rights were granted to those who were not entitled; but even worse, the form of the fierce monster has taken refuge in the heart of the merciful. How many times have the winds of our suspicions distanced us from our past loved ones?

You will not live long enough to make sure everything is correct, but I swear that you will live in peace if you start with pure intentions. Only then will you realize that you were right. If burdened by misgiving during your journey, you will return to your heart that never fails to mislead pure intentions, only to unmask your own misjudgments by yourself.

****

Do not be afraid to say anything, given that your intention has been washed with purity. Know that the soul's liveliness raises your heart's desire, and this signifies the race between the black and the white horse which symbolically represents the constant battle between good and evil. Deep inside yourself, you will know who you are when you question what you have done.

****

The intention is never to plant anything in a barren land, for the seed of a cowardly farmer will not grow and bear fruit there. Similarly, look into your soul to find fertile soil that will bear fruit. Do not be afraid then if you are determined and be sure that what is inside you is deep-rooted in your lively soul so that its branches reach high in the sky.

If you don't plant your intentions deeply and wisely, it will be uprooted from the surface of the earth and will never allow you to be stable.

****

4

**Respect yourself first and always,
this is the original human law.**

Try to sit alone in a café, watch the passersby and those sitting around you, then ask yourself what these people have in common; what differences do they have? What if their inside was disclosed to you and your inside was disclosed to them? How will you view them? What will justify your actions and behaviors from theirs?

****

You may like what you see in them but they may not like what they see in you. The question then is not about who likes what, but where does all of this originate from? It is the basis and logic, acceptance and rejection of the other. You may reject the other for his color, nationality, dress, or belief or you may accept him for the same reasons; but both judgments are unfair.

Therefore, there is a fair license that is given with tolerance for all human beings. It is called 'unconditional respect' and it applies to everyone. This card thought is based on the principle of acceptance of the other, as long as we respect ourselves and do not transgress, and as long as we are not harmed, even if some actions do not suit us.

****

From the very day of creation of the first man, our God has created the principle of co-existence and it guarantees that all will live in harmony, peace, and respect while at the same time have freedom of self-expression. Humanity continues to follow this principle, and if not, it would be lost.

$$**********$$

Don not compromise on respect, even if the delusion of doing good work sneaks into you. There is no good in many of our suspicions. These only grow out of pure egoism.

What is right for you may be more right for others, and what does not suit you may be impressive to others. They have what they want, and you have what you want, and so peace may prevail among you all if you are respectful of what they hold close to their heart and beliefs.

$$**********$$

5

Invest in energy of good news.

Good news can instill in you the spirit of positive energy, though you may not be ready to receive it.

****

If you receive good news, all you have to do is invest that exuberant spirit in you to accomplish a work that has been stuck for a while; then you will find yourself accepting the complexities of that work, and begin to look at that problem more easily until you get it done peacefully.

Try to lengthen the psychological comfort of good news by sharing your feelings with a loved one or a relative and describing and talking about the pleasure of such news to the utmost.

****

The joy that good news brings often ignites the enthusiasm of creative individuals giving spark to their thoughts. If you are one such creative person, never hesitate to propose and write down creative ideas, as creativity and innovation require a special temper that seldom comes.

****

Pleasure has 'vibrations' and 'halos' that change body chemistry; on the other hand, grief and melancholy have 'dreary vibrations' that destabilize the body. Therefore, write down your feelings of joy and pleasure with accuracy and deep description so that it may encourage and awake your determination in times of difficulty and distress.

****

6

Enjoy your retreat.

We may master the art of listening to those around us, but what is worse is when we begin to deduce and analyze the silence of others. When we feel what is going on in their inner minds, especially if they are among those whom we love or hate a lot, both alike, we must accurately ascertain the interpretation of such silence before concluding anything negative.

****

All this stems from a skill you have mastered well and that is concentration.

We all master directing our thoughts to what we desire until it is manifested in what is possible. Such a retreat of our thoughts is nothing new, but probably best forgotten.

Hence, the idea of retreats began with the prophets of God and the wise men of civilizations who directed humanity and all creatures resort to escaping quite often, sometimes from ourselves or our perceived limitations, and sometimes for false fun and comfort; but soon find ourselves alone.

At such moments, we find ourselves attracted to anything around us that makes an attractive sound and preoccupies our minds and thoughts so that the gloominess within us is silenced. Is this then our fear or hesitation to face reality?

****

The light of wisdom descended on the prophets and the enlightened while they were alone, without the need for anyone around them.

They directed their hearts by the language of silence and watched their breaths with pleasure and comfort without clinging to anything until they were accustomed to their loneliness.

They trained their careless and aggressive selves to live in tranquility until they had mastered the art of living in fruitful silence and wisdom.

****

Listen to yourself for a minute to live peacefully and happily next hour; retire for a day to enjoy the light of life, as wisdom does not come in the hustle, and silence is the language of beauty requiring no explanation.

The delight of an hour's retreat will give you a pure and tranquil sweetness that does not dry or fade for days.

When will you listen to the voice of your heart?

****

7

Admit your weakness, and then you will gain your strength.

You are a wondrous creation who combined weakness with power, through wisdom bestowed on you by the Creator; sometimes, you find yourself in the glare of your prime and sometimes broken and weightless like a feather in the air without any strength and unable to do anything.

****

You know yourself well and by knowing yourself, including your strengths and weaknesses, you create a path to a deeper knowledge of self. The next step is the complete acceptance of all that you are.

Certainly, focusing on excess weakness and disability in a person may blind the eyes so that one cannot contemplate and discover the sources of strength. In such a situation, contrary to what it implies, the first step is to admit weakness.

The first thing you need to do is to surrender yourself completely to the will of the Almighty so that you become powerless in His omnipotent presence. It is when you abandon yourself to His almighty power that you will begin to receive His divine strength and blessings. When the heart starts to get rid of the helpless weakness, it will become filled with hidden powers granted to you.

****

Here awakens the titan inside you, to begin a new stage that may be stronger than the one that preceded it when you stepped out of the hole and took one step forward. You will not fall again because you have stepped forward.

****

One important thing remains; it is the fact that you need to monitor yourself as a teacher, not a student. If you fall again, let yourself take advantage of the experience of previous weakness, then surely you will gain your strength twice and even more.

****

8

Living the moment and the secret of the perfect mood.

We all seek to achieve the highest levels of peace, the best state of mind, and the perfect mood if only all our times are filled with the happiness that we all aspire to experience.

However, we are soon separated from that status, because of the internal voices that surround our minds, and which precludes the attainment of serenity and purity which we all seek.

Many psychologists, as well as spiritualists, have asserted that living in the present moment is the first and last demand, but the real question is: What is this philosophy behind this thought? How and why does it work?

****

Living in the present time is a trick. You either think about the past and how things went, or you think about the future and how will things go?

That is the first disastrous escape from the present moment.

If the past is finished and the future is yet to occur, why are we preoccupied with them in the present moment of which we are a part?

****

Let's pause and contemplate the example of a pianist who is in love with his music to best understand the importance of truly living in the present.

The pianist, when he begins to play, pays attention to every sound, key, and note. He creates a beautiful melody that makes himself and others respond sub- consciously by elevating their mood and his very own during the process. At this point, he loses himself to the music, the mood, and the created ambiance, causing everyone who listens to vibrate to higher levels of emotion by forgetting everything and focusing on the present sensation.

How can this same pianist create such an ambiance with his music if his thoughts are elsewhere, with another person or situation, that distracts him from the complete abandonment required for his concentration? How could that perfect mood exist in his head when he is absentminded with various issues in his imagination while playing the piano?

So, it's wise to pay attention to your mood even if you play with your words!

9

Obsession comes dose by dose… Beware of getting addicted to it.

The heart, with its fluctuating pulse, is often obsessed with an anxiety that is surrounded by fear of the unknown or hopes that is surrounded by a promised joy. The heart is lost and listens to a sealed psychological talk, diving deeper into bottomless depths to end up seeing scenes confusing for fate and destiny.

****

Here comes the mind, whose role is to justify all those scenes with calculation and logic, to an extent that such a justification may drive the mind to almost believe that mirage is true water. You may follow the justification to prove that with the documented science you almost get internally confused, and here you can hardly retreat.

The soul, being a high and a pure divine breath, should not mislead you by its origin. If you trace it, your track will automatically alter as it does not give in or submit to harmful obsession but expels it with good hymns that do not meet in your original soul, because the original soul was created out of beauty.

****

How did that obsession sneak into you? And who allowed it to pass through you and burden your heart and then your mind until half of it was damaged, and almost reached your soul? Had you not heard your true buried voice, which has been living in you long ago? It is that part of yourself that you have not tamed yet until it becomes like a child with false joy.

If obsession knocks at your door, although it might appear like a wise advisor, know that it carries a dose of pain-saturated hope to make you an addict, in the sense that if you take the dose once, it will isolate you from everything that you know. Soon, you will feel the need for it and search for it to give you another dose until you become torn from within to such an extent that you forget how you became as such.

****

If you wake up with the knock and you find your heart bright with clarity, allowing you to see everything around you without the taint of a self-obsessed view, there's no need to worry. There is no existence of obsession, nor will it return to you as long as you refused it to enter into you, and just as bats live in dark caves and die in the bright sun, so too has this pain-saturated hope vanished at the break of dawn with the light of your pure soul, piercing through the false sense of self-entitlement, obsession, and the anxiety that comes with it.

10

Every day, you are a different person though inside you are one.

We experience different moods in a day because we are humans created from different components; earth, fire, air, and water. Each one of these components has its own different qualities; sometimes, you find yourself streaming and flowing like freshwater accepting everything and not disturbed or upset no matter how serious a situation; and sometimes you find yourself like a boiling kettle on raging fire that burns all who come closer. At other times, you find yourself profoundly thinking of an air bubble that separates you from the world and all that is known; yet other times, with your instinct toward laziness, languidness, and dullness, you look for everything that satisfies you with the least effort.

****

Naturally, we are as such in our different forms, but we are all originally one soul. If one quality overwhelms another, we feel dull and bored and may end up terminating some aspect of our lives before its natural time

****

Strangely enough, every day we hear and receive many calls and various signals from our inner and secret world; and sometimes, we receive red signs for every decision we have wrongly taken or intend to take. Nevertheless, the great surprise lies in every single opportunity which God inspires us by, and bestows on us each new day.

****

It is the opportunity of a new life, and the decision to rise up again despite the self-deception or laughter of others on our efforts and dreams. The happiness we experience with every new opportunity presented in every new day is similar to the feeling of an innocent child who lost his favorite toy only to cry for a moment and then continue with his day playfully with friends as if nothing happened. Do you know how this happens inside us? Have you experienced crying over a situation only to forget about it completely a few days, months, or years later as you realize and acknowledge your inner child's ability to forgive and forget?

****

It is a very simple equation.

In every situation you experience, a hidden voice emanates within you. Its source is you and your very self, seeking to be what you want, not what others want from you. It is here that you have the final words of what you will be so that you can make a comfortable and happy decision.

This monologue takes place in isolation from everything around you, and you are deaf about everything that may affect your decision.

If you go to the outside world, you will face a real test and will have a new opportunity to choose and seal your fate. Either you take the courage to achieve what you want yourself or you will be forced to do what others want; then you will be solely responsible for everything that happens to you because you yourself have chosen your fate and that presents itself as a new opportunity which decides the direction of your life.

This is exactly like the one who stands perplexed in front of the directions at the train station. The intertwined lines you see will not affect your choice of where you are now in your journey, but it will affect your destination.

The present stop will take you to the next station. So, although we are presented with multiple paths, everything may lead us to a different destination and we must resort to the voice within to decide.

What we really need in every perplexing situation of life is a new opportunity granted by the Creator so that we may become happier and more contented by the choices we make.

****

11

Describe yourself deeply and write it down…

From my own experience, I wrote my monologues and autosuggestions since many years ago, and today, when I read what I had written about myself, I find myself renewed and aware that I am following the right path, and that everything that comes in my way had been pre-planned for and matches the ends and desires of my life.

****

Although it is very difficult for a person to write about himself, it has always been the approach of great thinkers and wise men, who have been accustomed to document what they believed in. From the records of such moments in their daily life, they realized in retrospect that their life has remained invaluable, irrespective of age or time.

The difficulty lies in the first word that begins to describe your inner spirit and soul, your very hidden self. Then gradually, words flow one after the other, as you put pieces of yourself out in every word. Remember to make them simple, smooth, flowing, and connected to your true self.

This will bring you to realize your true and satisfied self, leaving no place for discontent and despair within.

****

When reading the biographies of great and renowned people, you will find a common language between them – a sincerity of expressions. Though such a quality may disclose their disadvantages; it prompts one to have spiritual purity as one can't wash ones' self unless he strips himself off of everything that covers his true inner spirit.

****

Finally, after you have finished describing yourself, you will see God's
graces pouring on you from all sides.

You were neglectful of His presence when you started this journey, but soon, you will begin to see the value of yourself and your affairs through the abundance of His graces bestowed on you.

When this new dawn commences, you will realize that you have been rewarded more graces now as compared to what you had when you arrived at the beginning.

****

12

When you are balanced, everything else will be balanced.

Matters may get out of your hand when you realize that you are stronger than before.

Perhaps, the very things that exhausted you and depleted your strength and power return only to wreck more havoc than before. However, just like mercury when released and which becomes stable once it regains its rounded bead-like form, you, too, will find yourself stabilizing only once you can find your natural state.

If everything is created with predestination, so too is your inner spirit waiting to return to its predestined state once you stabilize yourself by discovering who you are.

****

We, as rational creatures, seek to control, desiring for eternity; we chase the greater values, though this desire pushes us to trespass others' realms. When we reach the lowest depths and are almost consumed by the feelings of death, we leave all that we have owned and meet our basic instinct of survival.

****

Success belongs to him who knows himself well and does not hide behind false pleasures and distractions.

Whereas, the one who fills himself with mere joy and pleasure is eventually misled and disappointed.

On one hand, the scales of justice make you happy when you are aware of what is going on in the hidden threads that run deep inside you and control your movements.

On the other hand, when you are aware of the variables and perils around you that storm your sails, you remain more precautious of the scales weighing your deeds accurately based on what you do or don't.

How can you fill your scales without excess or arrogance? You will not know and realize the truth behind the things around you; you will give everyone his due right, without turning down a good deed that may delight others, nor do you overstate happiness that may make you small. If you are highly appreciated externally, check the truth of yourself internally.

****

When you open your eyes every day, receive the beautiful sunrise like a blessing and plan everything you want as you dream it to be. Then send the thoughts to heaven, adorned with all the beauty of your soul and with faith in the certainty that you will harvest good tidings.

If this manifests to you in your day, know that you are close to your heart and your Creator.

At this point comes the balance inside and outside of you, making you one with the universe as you witness abundance in your life.

13

Try the law of disregard, I don't say indifference!

You will not be able to encompass and embrace all things.

Certainly, you will not have all that you want. Even those who have fallen into the trap of the same situation have not been able to achieve what they wanted. This is the vortex of tension, attraction, control, and compromise.

****

With bitter rationalism and every beat of the heart, we realize that we will never achieve all that we want and desire. In other words, we will finally realize that there are other forces that manage things around us, despite our strength and determination, and we must leave enough room to submit and give in to these forces to calm down the internal engine that is constantly asking questions!

When you become weak and powerless, you won't give attention to your words, because you are ignoring everything around you except what regains your activity and vigor. That's why you have an instinctive readiness for the law of disregarding, and then you reactivate the components of your mind, but with greater devotion and more strength.

****

Do not pay attention to everything that is in your poor mind; let it pass. Yes, ignore things that are not a part of your destiny, but remember that it is unsympathetic to exhaust others in order to calm your mind and satisfy your desire because if you look at everything around you, you will find it going well as long as you do not talk and express your thoughts about every single matter.

****

You will lose, if you return once again, to the questions emanating from the dark tunnel of your inner self.

You may even find yourself surrounded by a torrent of ideas that you think will never change.

It is at this time that you must sympathize with your poor state of mind, especially when you fail to understand the extent of your invalid ideas, thoughts, or analysis.

That's when you should know that it's time to wake up because your thoughts of yesterday have now expired and are baseless and senseless in the current ties.

So, do not increase toxins in you; instead, free your mind to connect with your soul as it embarks on a new journey.

****

14

Let your soul travel ahead of your departure; live your soul's journey!

When I was young, I still remember the joyful atmosphere that filled the inhabitants of our small house just before the days of our journey or travel. It was a time when all preparations were done happily and with much hope until it was time to board the plane.

****

All those memories resemble the light-hearted spirit of a child, eager to reach his destination with excitement and anticipation. The atmosphere was one of special fun and happiness that added to the joy of the destination, going ahead of time to greet loved ones, as they waited for us.

****

Such memories reduce the distance between people, bringing each other
closer through imaginations and changing an aged old man into a rejoicing young child. until today, practice the same rituals before traveling, but now with a slight difference. With the revolution in social media bringing friends closer, we are keen to share and narrate the joyous dialogues about our travel preparations, creating an atmosphere of humor and fun, building anticipation and fun, and allowing us to live every moment through the joy of our soul.

****

Your keenness to raise the joys of your soul takes you to a state of permanent bliss. That's where your heart most welcomes the presence of friends, even if it involves traveling to seeing them and loved ones.

Recalling such travel dates and making plans to reunite with those close to your heart relieves you of heavy loads.

****

I was, and am still, keen to see the pictures of previous journeys which bring me much happiness.

Just try to go over old pictures or scenes that you were in, and then pour over them with satisfaction in search of everything beautiful in them and measure the impact of these silent scenes on you.

Certainly, these scenes will move mountains of overwhelming emotions and expressive words.

****

15

Stop the words "I'm not in the mood," you got yourself to make your day!

The mood is a box of different colors; if your hands reach into dark colors, they pigment your face with the same darkness, reflecting your dreary heart.

When you pick bright colors, they draw on your inner joy and accelerate your heartbeats for life, caring not about what may stop its blissful state of existence.

****

Why does our mood do this? Where did that feeling come from? How do you set yourself aflame and then whine after you were in the best mood? Are you looking for what may make you happier to rid yourself of distress? What would you do if you were powerless?

****

It is important to remember that we were first in a world of spirits before God created us from a mix of soul and earth, only to assume a body filled with wisdom to serve the Creator. When He created us, He deposited power in us; do you know what this power is?

It is the power of co-existence through renewed circumstances, despite extreme difficulty so that we continue to live together in peace and forgiveness.

What pleases and comforts the human heart most is the ability to continue every journey and maintain relationships through patience, tolerance, and renewal.

When a sense of happiness prevails, we are able to let it spill on those we meet. When we are sad, we ought to say; this too shall pass.

****

If you find yourself upset, it is helpful to think of who upset you and why? Perhaps, it is also important to ask if it was you yourself in any way or your own doings that have caused you to have a bad mood?

The one who uses his mood as an excuse to behave badly is like the one who puts locks on his life leaving all the keys neglected in a faraway drawer.

Remember that you alone are the one who can suspend your whole life for the mood of one uneventful day; and indeed, you alone are the one who can let the bad mood of a day pass to enjoy a life full of joy and happiness.

*** * * * * * * * * ***

16

Be brave and evaluate things well in your mind.

We may encounter moments that bring us into deep sorrow because of the abandoning of a loved one, or the rudeness of a relative or the ignorance of our feelings by someone important. However, with all of this, you remain the captain who directs the sails benefiting from the directions of winds and all circumstances that are happening around you and relying on your Lord first, and then on the capabilities of your soldiers onboard your ship, even though these winds of sorrow and pain are so powerful.

No matter how powerful the winds blow, your internal skills and courage will hold the sails, until the storm calms down gradually. At which moment, your mind begins to measure and appreciate things, the moment when the sea is tranquil. Remember that the brain does not work well under difficult circumstances, as it is the case with the ship in the middle of the storm.

****

The question here is, how can we courageously appreciate what is going on inside us? The answer is: tell me how much hope and positive energy you have, and I will tell you to what extent you can be brave.

****

The brave warrior does not win and will never win when he is defeated from inside, do you know why? Because if he thought and allowed the idea of defeat to sneak into him, he would be immediately defeated before facing the second enemy.

Since he was defeated before his first enemy, his inner self, inevitably he will not be able to win against the second.

All the motivational lessons in the world's top management schools revolve around one single idea: how to energize your internal forces for an external change.

The answer is to keep the flame of hope and the ambitious ideas burning in you under any circum-stances and to make this your first and final option.

Are you not aware of how a captain can encourage his sailors to cross storms, islands, and countries? Similarly, in order to be the captain of your inner thoughts and face them with courage, love, and hope to safely reach the shore, one must practice the same principle of inner motivation so that the scene of beautiful life on that new land will constantly serve as the needed motivation to accomplish your goals.

****

17

Be faithful...it is a fuel that never runs out.

Sometimes, you may go through a period of darkness, burdened by clouds of worry and suspicion against the one whom you love. For one reason or another, when this happens you develop a deliberate avoidance from the one you love and become indifferent to emotions only to cast a shadow of melancholy over your heart. It is only later that you will realize the destruction you have caused to the one you love by your baseless thoughts.

****

How did you dare do it? In fact, this question is like a dagger, its blade more fatal than anything because as lovers, we carry inside ourselves vivid scenes of the most beautiful situations that grow every day.

We water these memories with the love and faith of a pure heart which ought to be guarded against clouds of suspicion because love can never go under suspicious conditions.

****

You ought to resist the death of real love for the sake of a fulfilled life.

What if you didn't put up a good fight for a loved, loyal, and faithful one? How would you then give up on the energy of your life knowing that you didn't do all you could to save what you had?

Do not be surprised by excessive anxiety and the dreadful sleeplessness that comes only after reflection and in retrospect, for you would have missed joyful days for the sake of a brief period of darkness experienced by your soul.

So, be grateful to live thankfully for every single day we receive. All the lovers and the faithful beloveds have followed the path of faith that makes them the moments of true pleasure and gratitude and quench their thirst from rivers that never run out.

****

Remember that you are like other lovers; you may suffer what they suffer, long for what they look forward to, and dream as they do. Do not blame your heart, as it still holds pure love. Pure water comes out from under the ground and then rivers burst into endless deserts.

18

Do not pretend fun, but adapt yourself to it.

If you choose fun and its gentle waves, you may reveal other aspects of your personality. You will see that your laughter embraces the sky, and your heartbeats accelerate because of those laughs. Together, your heartbeat and laughter take you into a joyful world that makes you forget the horrors and woes of tomorrow which makes you an aged child.

****

You are on the threshold of the gate of the city of weddings, take off your shoes and enter confidently. Do you still wear your cloak worn by the dark thoughts that had almost destroyed you?

Get that cloak off and do not be afraid. Allow the stream of fresh air to renew your consciousness; the earth will not remember you while you are under darkness nor will the heavens cry for you when your soul rises there.

Do you see the colors that have been renewed around you?

How many roses are there before you now? Have you awakened from your dreary sleep?

If so, then it is wonderful now after your feet trod the land of love; do not look back so that those thoughts won't come to you. Speed up your steps.

****

Now, you are filled with fun; your mind and body have adapted to a different world.

Your consciousness will intensify with what is happening around it, and then you will feel that everything has been made for you.

You will realize that the fun hidden in you was blocked by your dark suspicions and now it is free.

Everything begins in and from your heart and from the very same heart you look at the reality of things.

****

A light shines from your heart, radiates out, and returns back inside. There is nothing more joyful than the fun of the heart, and nothing overshadows its purity. Look through a clear lens, with no disturbing thoughts and with no grief but with all joy.

19

Do not stop practicing your exciting hobby.

When we were young, we all shared a small game where we lived in a world of fun and endless merry, forgetting everything around us.

We were taken away from ourselves to a place where we did not know the meaning of a problem until we grew up.

****

That was our own world, where we lived every day with love, curiosity, and passion for the beautiful tomorrow, moving from one hobby to another until the night falls and its curtains came down.

Then you come back to the passion of waiting for tomorrow's fun, only to return afresh to your favorite hobby without boredom.

Be aware, my friend, today you are growing older; you have grown up and your kingdoms of concerns have grown along with you.

Do you remember your hobbies that were enchanted by your passion?

Do those hobbies still attract you today? Can you dare to practice them now? Please do not throw this task into tomorrow's basket, because you will soon pass this beautiful age and never be able to return to this time again.

****

Look at your old photos and then investigate the passion and memories of that exciting period. There, you will find the hobbies that ignited your creativity and it is time to greet them again in the golden hues of your youth.

Choose the ones that still bring joy to your soul and start anew.

****

You will soon hear the sounds of pure childhood and witness the youthfulness return within you. Keep those in you and start recalling the laughter of passion that filled your days and nights. The soul has no age nor does time; so, start with a new spirit and a heart that has been renewed by the water of happiness. Hurry up! Your companions are waiting for you!

****

20

Do not let go; pleasure is more in the little.

Sometimes, you may want to eat a creamy cake from a coffee shop that you visited on one of your travels. Even if you find it hard to do so, you just praise that delicious cake that pulls you back to that place. But, strangely, if you have the chance to try the cake for the second time, you will not feel those same wonderful feelings again.

What's the secret here for not wanting it as much as the first time?

****

The secret lies in the fact that pleasure is always in the little; let's feel the value of things, as over-experience and repetition lead to a desensitized pleasure of taste until it disappears, losing its real value. Just like caviar which is only served to the elite in a small dish and on a special occasion, so too must the experience of anything valuable be for it to retain its sense of taste and pleasure.

****

Human beings are created with enflaming desires and pleasure, and then they learned how to transcend them to greater pleasure – the pleasure of the soul. Nothing makes us satisfied all the time. We just follow the illusion that pleasure would continue.

****

Try to abstain from a habit that you repeat every day; for example, if you start your day without coffee and the next day resort back to your morning habit of drinking coffee, then taking a short break will bring you much pleasure when you return to your old habit.

Watch yourself as your face lights up while you sip your coffee. Such pleasure can only be enjoyed when it is deeply cherished with patience and understanding of the value of joy in little pleasures.

****

21

Do not separate your soul from your body and live the moment.

Sometimes you may find yourself swimming in another territory which almost feels like the heavens; you recall scenes from the deep past while waiting for a disturbing future.

However, on deeper reflection, aren't you sitting with your body at the same time and on the very same chair? Do you see your empty cup in front of you and wonder how you drank from it while passersby flocked around you?

****

Think about this experience a little deeper. Where have you really been? What happened to your body that separated it from your soul? Were you the same person who heard the girl laughing until the sound of her laughter grew so loud that time stood still for you? But then, she just left, and you remain standing where you were, unaware of her beauty or innocence.

Did you think about yourself during this experience? Were you aware of your presence and existence in that moment?

****

Every day is similar to such moments and wisdom lies in understanding such situations. These are scenes that are scrambling towards the horizon, but in reality, it is a cup filled with the harvest of every moment's interaction.

You are the adversary and the judge and, at the same time, you are the wise witness – either with a living body and an alert heart, or a living body with displaced thoughts and reasons.

****

How many times has a moment come to you but you did not live it out in all fullness? Often you were absentminded or delayed for some reason in your response to that moment and situation because of a distraction.

Every moment is a precious one in your life and so, you must live it fully or else will find that you will depart from this earth and such times will fly by before a more promising moment arrives.

There is no such thing as a perfect moment, but every moment is made perfect by your response to it.

****

Listen to your inner self and the voice within which calls you out. Reality is indispensable as it is linked to every experience of your soul.

Your body takes you to what you aspire and so, do not cut off the connection between your heart and soul. You are living your days out now, in this moment, attesting to every experience whether high or low, joyful or sad.

If your heart is awoken by a particular moment, do not postpone a beautiful word or a joyful expression from acknowledging it. Allow your mind and body to greet your inner spirit by its response and you will enrich each day better than yesterday.

****

22

Again. Learn how to love even if hurt by the one you loved.

To make a mistake once is not enough, what if you make a mistake twice? Do you submit to it the third time around? Then what if it is a loving mistake? Will you try again and again, or you will abstain while having the desire inside? The truth is, you are willing and hasty to some extent, especially when it comes to the things that make you weak and bring you a secret sense of joy.

****

Our Creator created our rise and fall. We laugh and grieve in one day; fear and feel safe in one night; love and hate the same person.

Indeed, such a complication is for the sake of life. The person we love may not be acceptable by the other; so too your heart may surprisingly find sanctuary with your friend's foe.

But life will never go on until love dominates over our wounds and pains.

If not, wars would continue unceasingly to crush hearts, people, and cities. You must love the one who hurt you, but this time in a different way. It should start from deep within a beautiful heart so that new nectar spreads; I will teach you how to do this.

****

Wars between countries end when weapons are set aside. Then, a dialogue begins and friendliness is respected. Everyone forgives and pardons the other and that's when love dominates, and rights are restored.

The same is with you as you will not be able to love anyone if you continue to hold your grudges and weapons against them, irrespective of whether you hold them for defense or revenge.

****

Start forgiving everything your loved one has done until you are healed and then your feelings will flow with beautiful purity and without obstacles. Then make your heart your guide and your first love as it is an endless source of giving. That is when you will be filled with love for all those you love without knocking their doors. Do not worry much about the love you give or get, for noble lovers are respected and often they have doors opened for them wherever they go.

****

23

Do you read? Please be honest.

I will not talk about the dilemma of reading and the aroused debate about the failure of our nation – the 'read' nation, which no longer reads. The final word is that there are no real figures or documented facts by the Arabs about the reality of reading, so I have a different talk about this beautiful addiction.

****

Look out for your friends, you will find them as books. Some of them are full of knowledge and you will need a while to digest their ideas while others are simple and live a simple life, that is repeated in the same manner daily. Still, there are others who search for more to find questions and answers guiding them towards newer horizons.

Here you find yourself in front of the real test, especially when you lose information and the figures to make a decision or even to contribute to it; eventually, you are in front of yourself realizing that you do not know anything new and the moment of truth comes to you: How long will you be ignorant of what is in those books?

****

I know many friends and relatives who can give dozens of excuses for not being able to read due to time constraints or difficulty; in fact, they do not know why they read, or how to read? There is a huge difference; the one who looks for the answers must be able to raise the question.

This stage will come but with patience and knowledge, and then you become knowledgeable because you now know something new.

****

Simply start and read a line then a paragraph; if you get bored, stop, and then go for page after page. If you get bored, close your book and put it next to you and then go back and refrain from reading until you get addicted to the situation. The sign of this is the desire to absorb new things including ideas, perspectives, scenes, and knowledge.

Then, you will live within those pages and cover the distances between your mind and imagination as you enter into a beautiful realm called the 'ecstasy of knowledge.'

****

24

Is your soul among the conjoined souls?

It is the company of friends with whom you find affability when you are free, with whom you feel at ease when you are annoyed or upset, with whom you forget heavy burdens of worries. When you meet them, you put aside the formality you were having the whole day; your soul mixes with theirs happily; while with them, you even forgot how long and how much you laughed and why.

****

With them, you live real moments. With them, you do not consider age differences; all of you have the same age because your souls are in harmony. It is the age of the soul far from the body with all the restrictions and borders it holds and this is the only thing that matters in a soulful friendship.

A soul that is preoccupied and fully engaged with the air of freedom – no considerations, nor apologies, is at a complete rebirth with itself.

Look at them with your heart, not your eyes, and you will find them like a pearl necklace where each bead lights the other beads with happiness and joy, and draws each other to be more cohesive in the face of horrors of the time. Inevitably, if you examined their feelings, you will find them holding feelings towards others that appear in situations and adversities.

****

The strange thing about this is that despite the difference and disagreement between them, it ends only with reconciliation and agreement. The tongue may slip, but the heart is reassured that it does not err. If anyone turns to his heart, he will find his soul twin which is also his dearest friend, calling him with a lofty love and saying, "I will not leave you, so do not leave me for my worries."

****

Part of the components of our daily lives is companionship and meeting with one another. Those who lose or miss companionship are found to be weak-hearted in the face of their affairs and their feelings. They simply close themselves up gradually and even refrain from seeking the advice of the wise. They become satisfied with their own sense of wisdom and righteousness.

****

25

Seek to fulfill your wishes though others may see them trivial.

Do you know the many of your wishes have not yet been realized in your life and have gone with the wind? You may mock yourself because your wishes and emotions have been simple and innocent. Yet, if you can imagine yourself with those lost wishes, you may compensate for the loss.

****

But wait, you may not realize that the passion for achieving wishes is rooted in your mind since the beginning of times. It does not matter if the lamp is lit or extinguished, as the spirit of things inhabits space and time and then creates ideas that form a beautiful world of wishes.

The wishes are part of your spirit; they mirror images of beauty held within you. Your wish of receiving a piece of candy may be achieved, then it gives you joy; what comes out of you is beautiful, but what is given to you is more beautiful.

****

Do not stop appreciating anything that elevates you. We all have different capacities. Our Creator gives out his gifts so that people will give a little bit of themselves to each other through selfless acts of kindness and compassion.

****

These gifts are akin to wishes and can be considered as precious gifts.

God deposited them in our days to achieve His justice. This is for granting us, the rich and the poor, full happiness in these times of our life. The rich look into the eyes of the poor to have comfort and happiness when they give freely what they have received freely from their Creator.

****

26

**Allow yourself to express all that you want...
Yes, everything you want.**

We sometimes make mistakes when we think that what pleases us at a certain moment should at the very moment please everyone close to us or around us. At the same time, we fail to withdraw ourselves from the depths of hidden sorrows and confusing images because we do not know where they came from.

****

Such is our careless self that does not rest as the Creator gave it the inspiration to see what was good and evil; so, you laugh and cry on the same day. Our atoms are full of sparks, eager for more, which may destroy it! On the other hand, prevention and deprivation purify our souls.

Have you ever been satisfied? If so, you will never get but a small fraction of all the glitter of the world, because others also have the right to have a part of it. The road has been paved for you to express all the confusion inside you as you do not know that carelessness is released through expressing it out.

****

There are many colors in your life that have formed metaphorical expressions about yourself; they form beautiful drawings or complicated knots that cannot be solved except by a pen or an artist's feather or fingers; so, never stop expressing yourself and freeing it.

It is very nice to accept the ups and downs of yourself with its fluctuation and changing colors at every moment. Then your waves calm down, and you can navigate without fear; and here lies the truth.

27

Choose for yourself a loved one whom you keep until the last breath.

The more you grow up, the more you iterate to yourself, "My life tape goes even faster than I expected it." Calm down as you will never be at the same pace with your fate because it is racing with time toward the horizon. But the whole issue is that beautiful scenes with loved ones around you slow down the speed of the tape and allow you to recover the taste of happy scenes again.

****

Do not be afraid, as everyone will be with you throughout your beautiful journey and will never let you wander alone. Only a few will be able to catch your hand and walk with you through difficult terrains. So, you too must look at them with your heart before your eyes, and then they will come closer to you until you find them present and helping you enjoy your time.

How hard it is to choose one of them because they are many around you, seeking to make you happy; and how easy to take your decision in choosing one, because he talks to you with a gentle heart; he gets closer before you knock his door and stands by his door ready and willing to welcome you with love.

****

Have you found him to be a beloved one or a faithful friend who carries the burdens of your day? Is he an inspiring person who enlightens your thoughts and the world? Is he the one who has given you pure love, until you become his beautiful world? If that is the case, congratulations; you are both great persons.

28

"We are together now," what about you?!

Where did the storms of your past problems go? How many of them remained in the tunnels of your poor brain? Have you found a single helping solution to your recurring questions? Or are you still immersed in your chemical analysis of the suspicions which dominate you?

****

So many are our fears are about tomorrow. The sages and wise men did not want to cure fear or eradicate it at all, because the fear of the unknown is rooted in our humanity and is part of it. It is where we seek eternity and desire for the fruits of tomorrow.

The secret lies in full vigilance and the consciousness of what you are now. Take a good look at everything around you and look with eyes that beat with our heart; stop watching the hands of the clock…time has gone!

****

Everything about you revolves around with predestination but do not worry, you are not responsible for it. It will go on with and without you, so listen carefully to the melody in your inner self. Only pay attention to what you are now in; nothing more unexpected will happen, so go with time!

****

We are together, we live in the beauty of everything around us and our love for them. That's when we are able to leave those who are drowned in time, miserably living in aging past, and suspicious of a lifeless future; they never knew the beauty of life or love in the present moment.

****

www.ingramcontent.com/pod-product-compliance
Lightning Source LLC
Chambersburg PA
CBHW070824170726
48000CB00019B/2472